A Note From Rick Renner

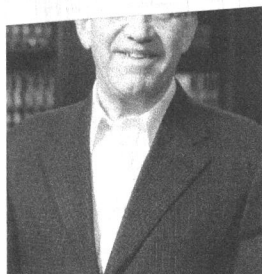

I am on a personal quest to see a "revival of the Bible" so people can establish their lives on a firm foundation that will stand strong and endure the test when the end-time storm winds begin to intensify.

In order to experience a revival of the Bible in your personal life, it is important to take time each day to read, receive, and apply its truths to your life. James tells us that if we will continue in the perfect law of liberty — refusing to be forgetful hearers but determined to be doers — we will be blessed in our ways. As you watch or listen to the programs in this series and work through this corresponding study guide, I trust that you will search the Scriptures and allow the Holy Spirit to help you hear something new from God's Word that applies specifically to your life. I encourage you to be a doer of the Word that He reveals to you. Whatever the cost, I assure you — it will be worth it.

> Thy words were found, and I did eat them;
> and thy word was unto me the joy and rejoicing of mine heart:
> for I am called by thy name, O Lord God of hosts.
> — Jeremiah 15:16

Your brother and friend in Jesus Christ,

Rick Renner

7 Things To Do Every Day To Stay Spiritually Strong

Copyright © 2020 by Rick Renner
8316 E. 73rd St.
Tulsa, Oklahoma 74133

Published by Rick Renner Ministries
www.renner.org

ISBN 13: 978-1-68031-719-0

eBook ISBN 13: 978-1-68031-720-6

How To Use This Study Guide

This five-lesson study guide corresponds to *"Seven Things To Do Every Day To Stay Spiritually Strong" With Rick Renner* (Renner TV). Each lesson in this study guide covers a topic that is addressed during the program series, with questions and references supplied to draw you deeper into your own private study of the Scriptures on this subject.

To derive the most benefit from this study guide, consider the following:

First, watch or listen to the program prior to working through the corresponding lesson in this guide. (Programs can also be viewed at **renner.org** by clicking on the Media/Archives links.)

Second, take the time to look up the scriptures included in each lesson. Prayerfully consider their application to your own life.

Third, use a journal or notebook to make note of your answers to each lesson's Study Questions and Practical Application challenges.

Fourth, invest specific time in prayer and in the Word of God to consult with the Holy Spirit. Write down the scriptures or insights He reveals to you about being filled with the Spirit and empowered by Him in your daily life.

Finally, take action! Whatever the Lord tells you to do according to His Word, do it.

For added insights on this subject, it is recommended that you obtain Rick Renner's books *Sparkling Gems From the Greek, Volumes 1* and *2*. You may also select from Rick's other available resources by placing your order at **renner.org** or by calling 1-800-742-5593.

TOPIC

Spend Time With God in the Morning

SCRIPTURES

1. **Psalm 5:3** — My voice shalt thou hear in the morning, O Lord; in the morning will I direct my prayer unto thee, and will look up.
2. **1 Thessalonians 5:17** — Pray without ceasing.

GREEK WORDS

1. "pray" — **προσευχή** (*proseuche*): close, up-front, intimate contact; coming close to express a wish, desire, prayer, or vow; used to depict a person who vowed to give something of great value to God in exchange for a favorable answer to prayer; portrays an individual who desires to see his prayer answered so desperately that he is willing to surrender everything he owns in exchange for answered prayer; pictures surrender
2. "without ceasing" — **ἀδιαλείπτως** (*adialeiptos*): without interruption; without an interval; without taking a break; continuously; can be translated "with no interruption, always, or persistently"

SYNOPSIS

The five lessons in this study on *Seven Things To Do Every Day To Stay Spiritually Strong* will focus on the following topics:

- Spend Time With God in the Morning
- Feed Your Spirit on Other Resources and Spend Time in Quietness
- Spend Time With Others Who Strengthen You
- Acknowledge God and Say No to Things You Should Not Do
- Be Refilled With the Holy Spirit

The emphasis of this lesson:

The greatest thing you can do to stay strong spiritually is to develop the healthy habit of spending time with God every morning.

Without question, we live in unique, challenging times. We are seeing and experiencing things that no other generation in history has gone through. Now more than ever, we need to be strong spiritually. The Bible says, "The strong spirit of a man sustains him in bodily pain or trouble…" (Proverbs 18:14 *AMPC*). In the midst of a very difficult season, Rick learned to incorporate seven essential habits into his life every day to remain strong in the Lord and in the power of His might (*see* Ephesians 6:10). These practices will strengthen you too.

The number one thing you need to do every day to stay strong spiritually is to *spend time with God*. There is no greater investment of your efforts and energy than to seek and soak in His presence! In God's presence is *fullness of joy* and at His right hand *pleasures forevermore* (*see* Psalm 16:11). So what does it look like to spend time with God daily? Is there a particular part of the day that He wants us to seek Him? And what can you expect to happen as a result?

Are You Reeling Under an Unrealistic Routine?

Like many believers, Rick Renner went through a very challenging time in his life many years ago. During that season, he and his wife, Denise, were pastoring two churches in two nations. This required them to fly in and out of the country every week. Imagine driving to the airport, standing in line to check your bags, going through security, and boarding a plane every three to four days, and then repeating the process again and again and again with no end in sight. Add to this the preparation, preaching, and pastoral ministry to the people that was required each week for two congregations in two different cultures, and you can see the overwhelming weight of the situation.

This grueling routine eventually began to take its toll on Rick. What was once exciting had become exhausting. He became drained physically, mentally, emotionally, and spiritually. Mindlessly he went through the motions of ministry like a machine set on autopilot. Then he reached a moment of crisis, and he and Denise did what they had encouraged countless others to do — they reached out to godly men who served as a covering of authority in their lives.

In an attitude of love and humility, these leaders spoke truth into the Renners' lives, pointing out that the schedule they were keeping was unreasonable and impractical. They urged them to make some specific adjustments in their lives in order to stay healthy and strong for the long haul that was ahead. It was during that trying time Rick recognized, developed, and implemented the seven things he needed to do every day to stay spiritually strong — and he still does them to this day.

To Make the Most of Your Day, Spend Time With God Every Morning

As we saw in the opening, the number one thing you need to do every day to stay strong spiritually is to *spend time with God*. And according to Scripture, that time should be in the morning. David — a man after God's own heart — said, "My voice shalt thou hear in the morning, O Lord; in the morning will I direct my prayer unto thee, and will look up" (Psalm 5:3).

David was a wise man who ruled as the king of Israel for 40 years, but he was not without problems. If you read the Scriptures, you'll see that he had struggles in his marriage relationships, with his children, with men on his staff, and with enemy forces who longed to see him destroyed. He knew that if he didn't pull away and spend time with God first thing every morning, he wouldn't make it. It is no coincidence that he said, "…O Lord; in the morning will I direct my prayer unto thee, *and will look up*" (Psalm 5:3).

The time David spent with God every morning enabled him to keep *looking up* instead of looking down. He knew the matchless power of seeking God's face first and being in His presence. It is no wonder he said, "But thou, O Lord, art a shield for me; my glory, and *the lifter of mine head*" (Psalm 3:3). God is the "lifter of your head" too, and when you spend time with Him in the morning, He will empower you to keep "looking up."

You may be reading this and thinking, *Well, I'm just not a morning person; I'm a night owl.* Although that may be true, it doesn't have to remain that way. With your willingness and God's grace, you can *become* a morning person in a very short time. Yes, it may require you to get up earlier, which means you will need to go to bed earlier. But staying up late doesn't add much to your life. Turning off the TV and your electronic devices and going to bed will probably keep you from a lot of trouble.

There is just something amazing that takes place when you choose to start off your day by giving God the "first-fruits" of your time. He will take the remainder of each day and multiply your effectiveness so that you will accomplish more than you thought imaginable.

Begin Your Day With Prayer

Everyone's personal time with the Lord will have its own unique flavor, but there are some vital ingredients that all of us must include. **Prayer** is one such ingredient. Rick shared how before he lifts his head off the pillow and puts his feet on the floor in the morning, he looks up to Heaven and begins each day with prayer. First he recognizes and welcomes the presence of God into his life. Then he begins to pray for his wife, his children and their wives, his grandchildren, his ministry staff and partners, his church members, and his TV family.

Although it may seem like these prayers would take a long time, they actually only take a few minutes. You may be surprised at how little time it takes to lift up your family members and friends by name and ask God to protect them and move in and through their lives.

Rick mentioned that after his initial prayers, he makes his way toward the kitchen and flips on the coffee pot. As he waits, he engages in a few minutes of exercise, which includes 75 pushups. One of the things he learned during his very difficult season when his life seemed to be falling apart was that staying physically fit adds strength to your spiritual life. The Bible says, "…Your body is the temple of the Holy Ghost which is in you, which ye have of God, and ye are not your own" (1 Corinthians 6:19). If your body is strong and healthy, it enables the Spirit of God to do so much more through you than if your body is sickly and out of shape.

Feed Your Spirit God's Word

Once Rick is done with exercising and has his cup of coffee, he makes his way into the TV room where he sits and begins to read his Bible. **Time in God's Word** is another key ingredient to spending time with Him every day. There is no other resource on the planet that is more valuable and life-giving than the Scriptures. You can read many other books, but the Bible is the only book that reads you.

Through the apostle Paul, God said, "The whole Bible was given to us by inspiration from God and is useful to teach us what is true and to make us realize what is wrong in our lives; it straightens us out and helps us do what is right. It is God's way of making us well prepared at every point, fully equipped to do good to everyone" (2 Timothy 3:16,17 *TLB*).

If you are serving in ministry, be very careful not to mistake your ministry preparation time for personal time with God. Many good people in ministry have fallen into this trap. You can be very busy doing things for God and end up spiritually malnourished and anemic from a lack of personal time in the Scriptures. You must take time to personally feed your spirit on God's Word. No one else can do this for you.

Many people ask, "What should I read?" If you want to receive God's wisdom on how to build healthy relationships, the book of Proverbs is wonderful. If you need healing in your emotions and want to experience deeper intimacy in your relationship with God, read the Psalms. If you desire a deeper revelation of who Christ is, read the four gospels — Matthew, Mark, Luke, and John.

Whatever part of Scripture you decide to dive into, pray before, during, and after you read. Ask the Holy Spirit — who is the Author of Scripture — to teach you what it means and how to apply it to your life. Don't rush or get in a hurry. Take your time to *read it, meditate on it, memorize it, and speak it*. Some days you may read a few chapters, and other days you may only be able to take in a few verses. Either way is okay. And if the Bible you are reading seems confusing or dry, begin reading a different version.

As you let the Word of God fill your eyes and ears, it will also flood your mind and touch your emotions. It will serve as a trusted guide in every decision you make and become an anchor for your soul that brings stability in the midst of life's storms.

Maximize Your Prayer Privilege

It is important to realize that prayer is not a daily activity you do once and then check off your list. Prayer is to be *a way of life*. In First Thessalonians 5:17, we are instructed to: "Pray without ceasing." This phrase comes from the Greek word *adialeiptos*, which means *without interruption, without taking a break*, or *continuously*. This doesn't mean we go through the day with our eyes closed praying from daylight till dark. It simply means we remain in an interactive state of communicating with God. We talk to Him and listen for Him to speak to us.

In Philippians 4:6 (*NLT*), the apostle Paul said, "Don't worry about anything; instead, pray about everything. Tell God what you need, and thank him for all he has done." And in Ephesians 6:18 (*AMPC*), he said to "Pray at all times (on every occasion, in every season)...." These verses let you know that you can...

- pray for your spouse and your marriage.
- pray for your children and grandchildren.
- pray for you leaders, including your pastor, your local officials, your governor, your president.
- pray for unsaved family members and friends to come to Christ.
- pray for financial provision and God's favor.
- pray for understanding and revelation of God's Word.
- pray for God's angelic protection at home and while you travel in the car, by plane, etc.

Don't wait until you are in a crisis to pray. You can pray about anything; anytime and anywhere. If something is concerning you, it concerns God. Begin to see prayer as a way of life that keeps you connected with your Creator who loves you and wants to be welcomed in every area of your life (*see* James 4:5).

Friend, don't ignore this proven word of instruction from God. If you truly want to be strong in spirit and rise above the enemy's snares, make a fresh commitment to begin spending time with God in the morning every day. Be open to allowing Him to do something brand new in your life. Make a decision to change the way you think and adjust your schedule to put Him first in your day. As you give Him top priority in your life, you will be amazed at how everything will begin to improve.

STUDY QUESTIONS

Study to shew thyself approved unto God, a workman that needeth not to be ashamed, rightly dividing the word of truth.
— 2 Timothy 2:15

1. One of the key ingredients to spending time with God is *prayer*. Take a few moments to reflect on these key passages from Scripture,

identifying prayer's importance and the power that is released when you pray.

- Luke 18:1; 1 Thessalonians 5:17
- Matthew 7:7-11; Luke 11:9-13
- Matthew 26:41; Mark 14:38; Luke 22:40
- James 5:13-18

2. *Time in God's Word* is another key ingredient to spending time with Him every day. There is no other resource on the planet that is more valuable and life-giving than the Scriptures!

- What do First Kings 8:56; Matthew 5:18; and Luke 21:33 all say about God's Word?
- In Second Timothy 3:16 and 17, what does Paul say is the overall purpose for God's Word?
- According to Romans 1:16; Hebrews 4:12; and James 1:21, what will happen when you choose to read and meditate on God's Word?

PRACTICAL APPLICATION

But be ye doers of the word, and not hearers only, deceiving your own selves.
—James 1:22

1. When you heard that the number one thing to stay spiritually strong is to spend time with God, how did you feel? Excited and energized? Or overwhelmed and condemned?
2. What are you currently doing on a daily basis to spend time with God? How does prayer and Bible reading fit into your life?
3. What practical steps can you take to expand and improve your personal time with God and make sure it doesn't get crowded out by other activities?

TOPIC

Feed Your Spirit on Other Resources and Spend Time in Quietness

SCRIPTURES

1. **2 Timothy 4:13** — The cloke that I left at Troas with Carpus, when thou comest, bring with thee, and the books, but especially the parchments.

2. **Proverbs 27:19** — As in water face answereth to face, so the heart of man to man.

3. **Psalm 37:4** — Delight thyself also in the Lord: and he shall give thee the desires of thine heart.

4. **Psalm 46:10** — Be still, and know that I am God: I will be exalted among the heathen, I will be exalted in the earth.

GREEK WORDS

1. "books" — βιβλία (*biblia*): plural, books

2. "parchments" — μεμβράνας (*membranas*): plural, parchments; membrane; used for writing or for taking notes

SYNOPSIS

In our first lesson, we learned that the number one thing you must do to stay strong spiritually is to spend time with God every day in the morning. As you give Him the first part of your day by spending time in His Word and in prayer, He will deposit into you His peace and His power. If you are afraid, discouraged, confused, sick, or worried, God stands ready, willing, and able to strengthen you and heal you through the supernatural power of His Spirit. As you draw near to Him, He promises to draw near to you (*see* James 4:8).

The emphasis of this lesson:

Along with spending time with God, every day spend time feeding your spirit on other resources and spend some time in quietness. These daily practices will empower you to stay spiritually strong.

Paul Fed His Spirit on Other Sources

In addition to spending time with God every day, it is also very important to *feed your spirit on other resources*. The apostle Paul knew this to be true and practiced it until the very end of his life. From a Roman prison cell, he penned his final letter to his young ministry apprentice, Timothy, and said, "The cloke that I left at Troas with Carpus, when thou comest, bring with thee, and the books, but especially the parchments" (2 Timothy 4:13).

There are two words that are particularly important in this verse. The first is the word "books." It is the Greek word *biblia*, which is the word for *books* in plural form. The second word of interest is the word "parchments." It is the Greek word *membranas*, which is also plural and it describes *leather parchments used for writing or for taking notes.*

While Paul was in prison awaiting execution, he had time on his hands. Rather than squander it with frivolous activities or give place to worry and fear, he requested books to read and parchments to journal his thoughts and what he was learning. If Paul — the brilliant scholar of Old Testament Scripture and writer of nearly two-thirds of the New Testament — knew he needed to feed his spirit on other resources and journal what God was showing him in order to stay healthy spiritually, we need to do the same.

Reading good books daily will nourish your spirit. Like fertilizer helps to nourish a garden, reading nourishes your mind and spirit and helps you grow at a faster pace. It has been said that readers are leaders, and it's true. Stagnate people are not typically people who read. Those who invest time reading life-giving resources are growing. Don't try and survive today on the fumes of yesterday's spiritual fuel. God has fresh fuel for you every day!

There Are Many Resources Available to You and Different Means To Take Them In

Some people will say, "I just don't have time to read. My life is too busy." The truth is all of us have some time to read; we just don't do it. We tend to make time to do what we want to do, which for many includes watching movies, listening to the news, surfing the Internet, playing video games, and scrolling through and posting on social media. Much of our leisure time is wasted on things that have no beneficial value whatsoever. Thankfully, if this is your case, you can change things by making new choices.

If you're not a reader, or you find it difficult to read, listen to good audiobooks. You can do this as you work around the house, exercise, or drive around town. Most people spend a lot of time in the car or in public transportation commuting back and forth to work. You can literally turn your vehicle into a university-on-wheels. As you drive, harness that time to listen to audiobooks or good preaching on podcasts or CDs.

The Internet is also a great source of teaching. You can look up anointed teachers and subscribe to their channels. You'll have instant access to their archives of messages plus be notified every time they post a new teaching. The method of taking in fresh, informative material is not important — just find what format works for you and begin to feed your spirit.

As the Lord reveals things to you, take time to write them down in your journal. Writing helps you remember what is most important and enables you to grow spiritually in a way like nothing else can. As you begin to write down the scriptures that come alive to you and the truths you are learning, your thinking will be refined, your beliefs will be established, and your faith will be strengthened. One word from the Holy Spirit can totally change the trajectory of your life.

Take Time To Be Quiet and Still Every Day

In addition to feeding your spirit on other resources and journaling every day, it is also imperative to *spend some amount of time every day in quietness.* Stop and think. Do you ever take time to be quiet? You need to — even if it is only for a minute or two. Times of quietness are like the white margins on a piece of paper. That blank space serves as a buffer to keep things in their place and avoid the chaos and confusion of life without downtime.

The Bible says in Proverbs 27:19, "As water answers face to face, so the heart of man to man." One reason people get confused and come under attack is because they get so busy they don't have quiet time, and therefore, are no longer in touch with themselves. In other words, they lose touch with what they believe, what they need, and what they feel. They just keep moving through life like a robot — which is exactly what happened to Rick many years ago. Deep contemplation is needed by all of us in order to stay in touch with our own hearts. When we are truly still, God allows us to see what is going on inside of ourselves.

Psalm 37:4 says, "Delight thyself also in the Lord; and he shall give thee the desires of thine heart." God will give you the desires of your heart, but first you have to know what your desires are so that you can ask for them. If you do not spend time with the Lord — and if you are not in touch with your own heart — how can you even know what to believe for?

Please realize — much activity without pause leads to spiritual dullness and confusion. That is why being quiet before the Lord is so valuable. You may be thinking, *Where in the world can I go to be quiet? I'm trying to raise a house full of children, and my work never stops.* If you don't seem to have a place to be quiet, consider one of these options:

- Going into the bathroom, shutting the door and locking it. If someone knocks on the door, tell them you're taking care of business (which you are) and that you'll be out in a few minutes. Then close your eyes and be still for a few moments.

- Sitting in your closet with the lights off or sitting in your car (engine off) in the garage.

- Taking a brief walk alone. The exercise will do you good — not to mention the fresh air and change of scenery.

- Getting up before everyone else is awake and sitting quietly by yourself.

Get creative and do what you need to do to have a few minutes of quiet, alone-time each day. Seize any moment you can to quiet your mind and emotions and cease from all activities. You need this for your spiritual, mental, and emotional health.

In Psalm 46:10, God says, "Be still and know that I am God...." Some revelations about God only come when you are still. And the full value of this quiet time cannot be taught; it can only be experienced. God told us to be still because we need it for our souls. The truth is, every member of your household needs this, so respect others in your home and give them the space they need to be alone. It will make them mentally and emotionally sounder and spiritually stronger as well.

To help you get started and develop a healthy habit of spending time in quiet stillness each day, consider carving out five minutes every day to be alone with God. You can even set a reminder and a timer on your phone. In those special moments, allow the Spirit of God to infuse you with strength as you still yourself in His presence.

STUDY QUESTIONS

Study to shew thyself approved unto God, a workman that needeth not to be ashamed, rightly dividing the word of truth.
— 2 Timothy 2:15

1. Have you experienced the value of feeding daily on other good resources? What books, audiobooks, podcasts, DVDs, or other teachings have made a deep impact on your life? What other resources are you currently using that you would recommend to a friend?
2. What does God say about the condition of our hearts apart from Him in Jeremiah 17:9? What good news does He give us in Jeremiah 17:10 (as well as Proverbs 21:1; 1 Chronicles 28:9)?
3. David knew the vital importance of spending quiet time in God's presence in order to know the condition of his heart. It was in one of those quiet times he wrote Psalm 139:23 and 24 (and Psalm 26:2). Take time to reflect on this powerful prayer and make it your own.

PRACTICAL APPLICATION

But be ye doers of the word, and not hearers only, deceiving your own selves.
—James 1:22

1. How often do you take time to be *quiet*? Would you say monthly, weekly, or daily? What does "quiet time" look like for you? Where

do you normally go to unplug from everything and be still? Can you name one positive, life-altering change or word of direction you received from God in a past quiet time?

2. Rick candidly shared how years ago when he was traveling, he wasted a great deal of time watching daytime talk shows and repeats of the daily news instead of preparing for preaching what God had called him to do. Can you identify with his situation? What "time waster" is the Holy Spirit showing you that you need to eliminate from your life?

3. To help Rick grow spiritually, the Holy Spirit told him to start writing books, which he was obedient to do. Do you sense God is asking you to be more proactive and constructive with your time? What steps can you begin to take to obey what He is telling you to do?

LESSON 3

TOPIC
Spend Time With Others Who Strengthen You

SCRIPTURES

1. **Hebrews 10:25** — Not forsaking the assembling of ourselves together, as the manner of some is; but exhorting one another: and so much the more, as ye see the day approaching.

2. **Psalm 54:4** — Behold, God is mine helper: the Lord is with them that uphold my soul.

3. **Ecclesiastes 4:9-12** — Two are better than one; because they have a good reward for their labour. For if they fall, the one will lift up his fellow: but woe to him that is alone when he falleth; for he hath not another to help him up. Again, if two lie together, then they have heat: but how can one be warm alone? And if one prevail against him, two shall withstand him; and a threefold cord is not quickly broken.

4. **Galatians 6:2,4,5** — Bear ye one another's burdens, and so fulfill the law of Christ. But let every man prove his own work, and then shall

he have rejoicing in himself alone, and not in another. For every man shall bear his own burden.

GREEK WORDS

1. "forsake" — ἐγκαταλείπω (*egkataleipo*): compound of ἐν (*en*), **κατα** (*kata*) and **λείπω** (*leipo*); the word ἐν (*en*) means in; the word **κατα** (*kata*) means down and out; the **λείπω** (*leipo*) means behind, as to be behind everyone else; pictures one who is discouraged, defeated, and depressed; depicts the emotions of a person who feels left out, down, depressed, and far behind everyone else

2. "exhorting" — **παρακαλέω** (*parakaleo*): to urge, beseech, plead, beg, pray; pictures one who comes closely alongside another person to speak to him, console him, comfort him, or assist him with counsel or advice; used to depict military leaders who came alongside their troops to exhort and plead with them to stand tall and face their battles bravely

3. "bear" — **βαστάζω** (*bastadzo*): to carry, lift up, or to bear something; to bear a responsibility

4. "burdens" — **βάρος** (*baros*): a weight that is heavy or crushing; could refer to a physical problem, circumstantial problem, or spiritual problem; a burden far too heavy to carry alone; if one attempts to carry it alone, it could be crushing

5. "every man" — **ἕκαστος** (*hekastos*): an all-inclusive term that embraces everyone, with no one excluded

6. "burden" — **φορτίζω** (*phortidzo*): a load that is normal and expected for every individual to carry; military term to describe the backpack that every soldier was required to carry as a part of his career as a soldier; a heavy load that could not be avoided

SYNOPSIS

So far we have examined three things we need to do every day to stay strong spiritually. The first one needed is to *spend time with God every day*. This includes looking up to Him in prayer first thing in the morning — and all throughout the day — as well as spending time reading His Word.

The second healthy habit is to *spend some amount of time every day feeding yourself on other resources*. This nourishes your mind and your spirit just like fertilizer nourishes a garden and helps it grow faster and produce more fruit.

This brings us to the third practice to stay spiritually strong, and that is to *spend some amount of time every day in quietness.* So many people move throughout their day at break-neck speed, never taking time to press pause on life and just be still. Consequently, they are out of touch with themselves; they don't know what they believe, how they feel about things, or how to pray.

God has commanded us to "Be still, and know that I am God..." (Psalm 46:10). When we are quiet and still, He enables us to see our own heart. He lets us get in touch with what we believe, what we are feeling inside, as well as the attitudes and issues we need to confront.

These activities are to be done every day. The more you do them, the more they will become second nature — like brushing your teeth, taking a shower, and getting dressed each morning. And the good news is they only take minutes to do!

The emphasis of this lesson:

Another vital practice to staying spiritually strong is to spend some amount of time with people who strengthen your soul every day.

If you recall in Lesson 1, we saw how Rick had taken on a schedule that was unrealistic and impractical and it had left him depleted mentally, emotionally, physically, and spiritually. He was taking care of everyone else at two churches in two different countries, but he wasn't taking care of himself. With the exception of his precious wife Denise, no one was pouring back into him and replenishing him like he was doing for others. This was a practice that desperately needed to change.

The Holy Spirit revealed to Rick the fourth healthy habit to stay spiritually strong, and that is to *spend some amount of time every day with people who strengthen your soul.* This is especially true for those who are responsible for a large number of other people and have many daily duties and tasks. Stop and think. Do you have a relationship with someone who is pouring into your life? Is there someone looking after you and speaking into your life daily the way you do for others? If you don't have someone, you need someone.

Don't 'Forsake' the Friendship of Others

The Bible talks about being accountable to others in many places including Hebrews 10:25. It says, "Not forsaking the assembling of ourselves together, as the manner of some is; but exhorting one another: and so much the more, as ye see the day approaching."

Notice the word "forsake." It is the Greek word *egkataleipo*, which is a triple compound of the words *en*, *kata*, and *leipo*. The word *en* means *in*; the word *kata* means *down and out*, and the word *leipo* means *behind*, as *to be behind everyone else*. When these three words are compounded, it pictures *one who is discouraged, defeated, and depressed*. It depicts *the emotions of a person who feels left out, down, depressed, and far behind everyone else*.

Does that sound like anyone you know? Does it describe *you*? Sadly, most people stop going to church and withdraw from close fellowship with others when they feel *forsaken*. When they need comfort, encouragement, and loving correction the most, they avoid the very people who can give it to them. Friend, you need to be actively connected in a local church. You need the support structure of trusted friends who truly care and will speak the truth in love to you — *especially* when you feel discouraged, defeated, and depressed.

Receive the 'Exhorting' of Your Close Companions

Instead of forsaking our assembling together, God says we are to be "exhorting one another." The word "exhorting" in Greek is the word *parakaleo*, which means *to urge, beseech, plead, beg*, or *pray*. It pictures *one who comes closely alongside another person to speak to him, console him, comfort him, or assist him with counsel or advice*. This word was used to depict military leaders who came alongside their troops to exhort and plead with them to stand tall and face their battles bravely.

Again, stop for a moment and think — who in your life comes closely alongside you to speak into your life, to console you, to comfort you, and to assist you with counsel or advice? Who urges you, pleads with you, and begs you, to stand tall and face your battles bravely? Can you identify this person — or these people — in your life?

These are people who watch over your soul. They speak into your life, talk with you, pray with you, and speak the Word over you. They hold you accountable for your attitudes and actions, and the relationship you have with them is *reciprocal*. In other words, what they provide for you, you provide for them.

Men, you need other men, and ladies, you need other ladies in your life. You need people who will encourage you when you're down and who will lovingly point out when you're wrong. These are individuals who have no hidden agenda — they simply desire to invest in you and pour into your soul because they genuinely love you and want you to succeed.

Here Are Some Simple Steps for Starting and Sustaining Meaningful Relationships

By now you may be wondering, *How in the world can I spend time every day with people who strengthen my soul? Is that even doable?* The answer is yes, it's doable. It all starts with **praying for God-connections**. Most importantly, ask the Lord to help you identify people you can *trust*. These individuals are a "safe place" for you — people with whom you feel comfortable confiding in that you know will not share your business with others. Second, they are willing to be in covenant with you and *available*.

Once you have identified these people, don't wait for them to contact you. **Take the initiative and reach out to them.** Ask them about being in covenant relationship together on a daily basis, and then do your best to stay connected every day, which is not as difficult as you may think.

You can stay connected daily by sending a text message, an email, or a phone call. You can also take advantage of today's technology and communicate through the Internet using Skype or Zoom. The conversation or text doesn't have to be long. It just needs to be truthful. If you're doing well, let them know it. If you are in a depleted state, tell them. The truth of the matter is, the more you get to know each other, the more readily you will be able to detect when something is wrong.

God Ministers to You and Meets Your Needs Through Others

Make no mistake: God is totally for you having meaningful relationships like these! Although some people will say, "I don't need anybody. I've got God, and He's all I need," that is not true. Look at what David said in Psalm 54:4: "Behold, God is mine helper: the Lord is with them that uphold my soul."

Did you catch the second part of that verse? It says, "...*the Lord is with them* that uphold my soul." So in addition to God being our Helper, He is also working through the people He has placed in our lives to "uphold our soul."

Indeed, there is power released when we come together with others. Solomon, David's son understood this principle very well and wrote one of the most compelling passages on the subject. He said: "Two are better than one; because they have a good reward for their labour. For if they fall, the one will lift up his fellow: but woe to him that is alone when he falleth; for he hath not another to help him up. Again, if two lie together, then they have heat: but how can one be warm alone? And if one prevail against him, two shall withstand him; and a threefold cord is not quickly broken" (Ecclesiastes 4:9-12).

Once again, ask yourself, "Who is upholding my soul? Who am I working with that can share in the rewards of my labor? Who is standing with me to help me up if I fall?" You need close relationships like this in your life. Forming associations like these is one of the smartest things you will ever do.

We Are Called To 'Bear One Another's Burdens'

In the New Testament, we find that the apostle Paul also gave valuable input on relationships. In Galatians 6:2 he said, "Bear ye one another's burdens, and so fulfill the law of Christ."

The word "bear" is the Greek word *bastadzo*, which means *to carry, lift up, or to bear something; to bear a responsibility*. The word "burdens" in Greek is the word *baros*, and it describes *a weight that is heavy or crushing*. It can refer to *a physical problem, circumstantial problem, or spiritual problem*. It is *a burden far too heavy to carry alone*.

If a person attempts to carry a *baros* (burden) alone, it could be crushing. We have the responsibility to help others carry and walk through overwhelming situations that they cannot carry on their own. When the Lord makes us aware of someone who is under a very heavy burden, He is calling us to come alongside them and help them carry it.

Now this doesn't mean we are to carry everyone's problems or that others are to carry all our problems. It means we are to help one another shoulder the burdens that are unbearable. The apostle Paul confirms this a couple verses later. He said, "But let every man prove his own work, and then shall he have rejoicing in himself alone, and not in another. For every man shall bear his own burden (Galatians 6:4,5).

The words "every man" is the Greek word *hekastos*, and an all-inclusive term that embraces *everyone, with no one excluded*. What's interesting is the word "burden" in verse 5 is different than the one in verse 2. Here the word "burden" is the Greek word *phortidzo*, which describes *a load that is normal and expected for every individual to carry*. This is *a military term to describe the backpack that every soldier was required to carry as a part of his career as a soldier.* It depicts *a heavy load that everyone must carry that could not be avoided.* Hence, there are some things in this life that cannot be avoided that we must carry alone. These personal responsibilities include things like working to provide for one's needs, paying one's bills, maintaining a personal relationship with God, using one's gifts to serve others, and tithing.

Friend, don't buy the lie that you can do life alone. You need people in your life — strong people — to help you do what God has called you to do. And you need to connect with them every day. In our next lesson, we will look at two more important things you need to do every day to stay spiritually strong.

STUDY QUESTIONS

Study to shew thyself approved unto God, a workman that needeth not to be ashamed, rightly dividing the word of truth.
— 2 Timothy 2:15

1. The strength of a good friend is priceless! The richness of one's life is not measured by the amount of money and material possessions one amasses. It is measured by the quality of relationships he or she develops. God's Word has much to say on the subject. Carefully read these passages and share the insights the Holy Spirit shows you.
    - **Ecclesiastes 4:8-12**
    - **Proverbs 13:20**
    - **Proverbs 17:17**
    - **Proverbs 27:17**
    - **John 15:13**

PRACTICAL APPLICATION

> But be ye doers of the word, and not hearers only,
> deceiving your own selves.
> — James 1:22

1. More than likely, you are avidly taking care of others, pouring into them spiritually and helping to meet their daily needs. The question is, "Who is pouring into you?" Who is strengthening and replenishing your soul? Whose voice speaks into your life on a regular basis, asking you how you are doing and telling you when you are off track? (Write as many names that come to mind.)

2. How often do you connect with them and what methods seem to work best? Is your relationship reciprocal — do you give and receive each other's assistance equally?

3. Looking back over your times together, name at least one situation in which your friend gave you counsel or assistance that undeniably changed the course of your life. Likewise, share an occasion in which your counsel and assistance visibly impacted their life. (If you're not sure, give them a call and ask them. This is a great opportunity to encourage and strengthen one another.)

LESSON 4

TOPIC

Acknowledge God and Say No to Things You Should Not Do

SCRIPTURES

1. **Psalm 119:164** — Seven times a day do I praise thee because of thy righteous judgments.

2. **Psalm 19:12,13** — Who can understand his errors? cleanse thou me from secret faults. Keep back thy servant also from presumptuous sins; let them not have dominion over me: then shall I be upright, and I shall be innocent from the great transgression.

GREEK WORDS

There are no Greek words included in this lesson.

SYNOPSIS

In our first three lessons, we discovered four of the seven things we need to do *every day* to stay spiritually strong throughout one's lifetime. They are:

1. Spend time with God in the morning.
2. Spend time feeding your spirit on other resources.
3. Spend some amount of time in quietness.
4. Spend some amount of time with those who strengthen you.

These are healthy habits that are not difficult, nor do they require a great deal of time. But when you put them into practice, they will serve as life-giving medicine to your spirit and soul, just as they did in Rick's life and in the lives of countless other believers.

The emphasis of this lesson:

The fifth and sixth things you need to do every day to stay spiritually strong is to take time to stop throughout your day to acknowledge God and learn to say "no" to the things you are not supposed to do.

Take Time To Stop Throughout the Day To Acknowledge God

As we learned in our first lesson, David was a man anointed by God to serve as the king of Israel. At the same time, the Bible tells us he had many enemies — both outside and inside his home. A careful reading of the book of Psalms indicates that this man of great passion had to learn how to control his emotions and his thinking. He kept himself spiritually strong by spending time with God in the morning every day — which is our number one thing to do — and by putting into practice the fifth empowering habit, which is to *take time to stop throughout the day to acknowledge God.*

In Psalm 119:164, David said, "Seven times a day do I praise thee because of thy righteous judgements." Although he was surrounded by injustice, he made it a point to praise God again and again. He learned to stop seven times throughout the day and acknowledge God, saying things like, "God, You are still on the throne and in control of my life. Regardless of all the unrighteous people scheming around me, You are in charge and are going to do right by me." By stopping to acknowledge God's justness, David reminded himself of God's goodness and kept his mind and emotions under control, and the same thing will happen to you.

You may be thinking, *How can I remember to stop seven times a day to acknowledge God?* It is actually not as difficult as you may think — especially in light of today's technology. One of the easiest ways to remind yourself to stop and acknowledge God is to set an alarm or reminder on your phone to go off throughout the day. Each time it sounds, take a moment to pause and verbally recognize that God is still on the throne and that He has everything under control. You can declare things like:

- "God, You are all-powerful and nothing nor anyone is stronger than You (*see* First Chronicles 29:12). I will not be taken down by this situation."

- "God, You are all-knowing; You see everything going on in my life and in the entire world. You have delivered me from problems in the past, and You will deliver me from the things I'm currently facing" (*see* Hebrews 4:13; Psalm 37:17).

- "God, my times and my life are in Your hands. No one can touch me or take me down as I rest and trust in You" (*see* Psalm 31:15; John 10:28-30).

Acknowledging God in this way takes less than a minute, and it's easy to do. Simply declare what the Bible says about Him in spite of your challenging situation or how you feel. This is what David meant when he said, "O magnify the Lord with me, and let us exalt his name together" (Psalm 34:3). When you magnify the Lord, you acknowledge His goodness on purpose, and thus minimize the problem.

This purposeful recognition that God knows all, sees all, is all-powerful, and will do right by you is what the apostle Paul meant when he said, "Set your affection on things above, not on things on the earth" (Colossians 3:2). In Greek, the phrase "set your affection" means *fix your thoughts*. Your mind will never automatically begin focusing on eternal, heavenly things. Therefore, you must purposefully harness your thoughts and bring them in to alignment with God's Word. If you will learn to develop this practice every day, God's peace will flood your mind and emotions, and your life will take on new meaning.

Every Day Say "No" to the Things You Are Not Supposed To Do

The sixth thing you need to do every day to stay spiritually strong is *to say "no" to the things you are not supposed to do*. To understand this valuable truth, we turn once more to the book of Psalms and the writings of David. He prayed to God saying, "Who can understand his errors? cleanse thou me from secret faults. Keep back thy servant also from presumptuous sins; let them not have dominion over me..." (Psalm 19:12,13).

Notice David asked God in verse 13 to keep him from committing "presumptuous sins." These are sins committed by good men and women, if left to themselves. Essentially, it is the sin of assuming you are to do something *without* praying and asking God about it. For example, you hear about a financial need that a family has, and you automatically presume you are to meet that need. Without stopping to pray and asking God what you should do, you pull your money together and take care of the need on your own. This is a "presumptuous sin."

Rick shared that out of the seven things to do to keep ourselves spiritually strong, avoiding presumptuous sins was the hardest. For years he assumed that he was to take care of *every* need that came in front of him, so he became consumed by responsibilities God never intended Him to have. Eventually, he came to the realization that *pride* was keeping him from saying "no" to people. He wanted to be able to meet everyone's needs and win their approval, but he nearly lost his life in the process. Sound familiar?

The truth is that 85 percent of what you do, someone else can do; and ten percent of what you do, someone else can be trained to do. Only about five percent of what you do can only be done by you, and that is where you need to focus your efforts and energy. Sadly, many people aren't doing the 5 percent that only they can do because they are too busy doing the 85 percent that someone else can do or the 10 percent that someone else could be trained to do. They have said "yes" to many things they should have said "no" to, and their presumptuous sins are dominating their lives.

Back in his early years of ministry, Rick did everything regarding his ministry. He attended all the staff meetings and was involved in every decision that needed to be made. Nothing happened without his involvement or attention. Yet God had surrounded him with incredibly gifted people who were very capable of handling things on their own. In fact, they were able to do many of the things he was doing better than him. Unfortunately, because he had his hands in everything, he was preventing them from fulfilling their call. Once he learned to let go, the ministry was positioned to grow. He is now able to focus his attention and energy on the five percent that only he can do: communicating through writing and teaching, and leading churches and a media ministry.

If your hands have to touch everything, you'll never grow very far because you can only reach so far. Look around you. Who has God placed in your life to help you get things done? This same principle applies in your home as well. If you will learn to let go of trying to manage everything and stop saying "yes" to things God is asking others to do, your life will be much more peaceful and more productive.

Friend, don't feel obligated to financially give to every cause or serve on every project you hear about. Before you commit, stop and pray and ask God what He wants you to do. If you don't sense God's prompting to get involved, just say "no." You are not called to do everything or be everything to everybody. If you are saying "yes" to everything all the time, someone else is being robbed of the opportunity to stretch and grow their gifts. As you learn to say "no" to what God has not called you to do, you are liberating others to flow in their gifts.

STUDY QUESTIONS

**Study to shew thyself approved unto God, a workman that needeth
not to be ashamed, rightly dividing the word of truth.
— 2 Timothy 2:15**

1. According to God's Word, how important is being *thankful* and *giving praise* to God? (Consider Psalm 100:1-5; 103:1-3; 150:6; Hebrews 13:15; and First Thessalonians 5:18.)

2. A great way to cultivate a heart of praise and thankfulness toward God is to practice thinking about all the good things He has done — and is doing — in your life (*see* Psalm 77:11,12). Take a journal or a

notebook and begin making a list of His blessings and faithfulness to you. When you begin to feel overwhelmed or discouraged, pull out that list and start thanking Him.

Make a list of…

- the unexpected, undeserved blessings God has provided.

- all the times He has protected you from what could have been disastrous.

- the times He has been patient with you and forgiven your sins.

- the good people He's placed in your life to support you, pray for you, and speak into your life.

3. Carefully read back over your answers in Question 2 and attach any related scripture verse that comes to mind for each event. Then write out a personal declaration with which you can begin to praise God for throughout each day.

PRACTICAL APPLICATION

**But be ye doers of the word, and not hearers only,
deceiving your own selves.
—James 1:22**

1. Years ago Rick assumed that he was to take care of every need that came in front of him. As a result, he became consumed by responsibilities God never intended Him to have. *Pride* was keeping him from saying "no" to people. He wanted to be able to meet everyone's needs in order to win their approval. Do you find it difficult to say "no" to helping people? In what ways can you identify with Rick's dilemma?

2. About 85 percent of what you do, someone else can do; and ten percent of what you do, someone else can be trained to do. The remaining five percent of what you do can only be done by you. Can you identify this five percent in *your* life — the activities where you need to focus your efforts and energy? What are you currently doing that you know in your gut you need to let someone else do — or train someone to do? Is there a project or commitment you are about to say "yes" to, but in your heart you know you are supposed to say "no" to? If so, what is it?

TOPIC
Be Refilled With the Holy Spirit

SCRIPTURES

1. **Ephesians 5:15-18** — See then that ye walk circumspectly, not as fools, but as wise, redeeming the time, because the days are evil. Wherefore be ye not unwise, but understanding what the will of the Lord is. And be not drunk with wine, wherein is excess; but be filled with the Spirit.

2. **Philippians 1:19,20** — For I know that this shall turn to my salvation through your prayer, and the supply of the Spirit of Jesus Christ. According to my earnest expectation and my hope, that in nothing I shall be ashamed, but that with all boldness, as always, so now also Christ shall be magnified in my body, whether it be by life, or by death.

GREEK WORDS

1. "walk" — περιπατέω (*peripateo*): to walk around; to habitually walk; and it also referred to one's lifestyle; Paul was calling them to move up higher and to begin living a new lifestyle

2. "circumspectly" — ἀκριβῶς (*akribos*): accurately, carefully, or exactly

3. "fools" — ἄσοφος (*asophos*): unenlightened or unintelligent

4. "redeeming" — ἐξαγοράζω (*exagoridzo*): compound of the Greek words (*ex*) and (*agoradzo*); the word (*ex*) means "out"; the word (*agoradzo*) means "I buy"; to buy back, to redeem, or to make the most of

5. "unwise" — ἄφρων (*aphron*): unintelligent or brainless

6. "understanding" — συνίημι (*suniemi*): a coming together; putting all the pieces together, like putting together the many pieces of a jigsaw puzzle to reveal the big picture

7. "drunk" — μεθύσκω (*methusko*): to excessively drink alcohol; a drunkard "filled" — πληρόω (*pleroo*): to fill to capacity; to fill to the full; the tense indicates perpetual activity — be BEING filled; we are to be continually filled with the Spirit

8. "supply" — ἐπιχορηγία (*epichoregia*): a lavish provision; an outrageously large contribution; a massive contribution

9. "magnified" — μεγαλύνω (*megaluno*): amplify; boost; enlarge; expand; increase; make great; magnify

SYNOPSIS

Just as your body needs daily care and attention to be energized and strong, so does your spirit. Thus far, we have identified six of the seven proactive steps you can take every day to stay strong spiritually, and they are:

1. Every day spend time with God in the morning.
2. Every day spend time feeding your spirit on other sources.
3. Every day spend some amount of time in quietness.
4. Every day spend some amount of time with those who strengthen your soul.
5. Every day take time to stop throughout the day to acknowledge the presence of God in your life.
6. Every day say "no" to the things you are not supposed to do.

As you begin to incorporate these practices into your life day after day, month after month, and year after year, the positive impact they make will be simply amazing! These healthy habits will keep you on track and make you vibrant spiritually, mentally, emotionally, and physically. There is one more thing you need to do every day to stay strong spiritually, and that is every day — without exception — *pray to be refilled with the Holy Spirit.*

The emphasis of this lesson:

The baptism in the Holy Spirit takes place once in a person's life, but after that there are countless re-fillings we can receive. Praying to be refilled with the Holy Spirit every day is one of the most important things you can do to stay spiritually strong.

In Acts Chapter 2, the Bible documents the historic Day of Pentecost when the Holy Spirit invaded the Upper Room in Jerusalem and began to take up permanent residence inside of believers. One hundred and twenty Christ-followers had gathered there — including Peter and John — when suddenly they were all filled with the Holy Spirit (*see* Acts 2:1-4). A short time later, Peter and John were arrested for teaching in the name of

Jesus and brought before the religious leaders. As they stood in front of the Jewish Sanhedrin, the Bible says Peter and John were "filled with the Holy Spirit" (*see* Acts 4:8). In Greek, this actually says, "just then, at that moment; being filled with the Spirit." In other words, in that instant they were refilled with the Spirit.

When you come to the end of Acts 4, just hours later, these same two men — along with the other faithful followers of Jesus who were praying in the Upper Room — were once again refilled with the Holy Spirit (*see* Acts 4:31). Although there is only one baptism in the Spirit, there are many infillings, and God wants to refill you with His Spirit every day.

The Church of Ephesus Started in the Power of the Spirit but Fizzled in Its Fervor Over Time

History reveals that the church of Ephesus had been birthed in the mighty power of God, and they continued in His power for many years. The apostle Paul — along with his ministry partners Aquila and Priscilla — began teaching in the renowned School of Tyrannus, which was right in the central part of Ephesus. People from all across Asia began coming to that school every day, six days a week. And the Bible says, "This continued by the space of two years; so that all they which dwelt in Asia heard the word of the Lord Jesus, both Jews and Greeks. And God wrought special miracles by the hands of Paul" (Acts 19:10,11). These miracles had never happened anywhere else. Indeed, the church of Ephesus was moving mightily in the power of the Holy Spirit!

But over time, this influential, Spirit-filled church began to experience some really difficult issues which Paul addressed in Ephesians 4. The people were backbiting, lying, gossiping, and acting with malice, and it was grieving the Holy Spirit. Their behavior had opened a door for the devil to enter and it was causing many problems. These believers needed a new encounter with the Holy Spirit and a fresh infilling of His presence.

Paul Brought Correction to the Ephesian Believers

In Ephesians 5:15, Paul said, "See then that ye walk circumspectly, not as fools, but as wise." The word "walk" in Greek is the word *peripateo*, which is a compound of the word *peri*, meaning *around*, and the word *pateo*, meaning *to walk*. When these words are compounded to form the word *peripateo*, it means *to walk around* or *to habitually walk*. It can also refer to one's *lifestyle*. Hence, Paul was calling the Ephesian believers to move up higher and to begin living a new lifestyle.

Specifically he told them to walk "circumspectly," which is the Greek word *akribos*, and it means *accurately, carefully, or exactly*. He also urged them to be wise, not fools. The word "fools" is the Greek word *asophos*, from the word *sophos*, which means *enlightened* or *intelligent*. In this case, because there is an "a" attached to the front of it, the meaning is reversed. Thus, Paul urged them not to be *unenlightened* or *unintelligent*.

Putting the meanings of all these words together, here is the *Renner Interpretive Version (RIV)* of Ephesians 5:15:

> **Quit all this foolish behavior and stop acting unintelligent. Begin acting like the intelligent, cultured believers I know you can be.**

To walk in wisdom, Paul encouraged them to be, "Redeeming the time, because the days are evil" (Ephesians 5:16). The word "redeeming" is the Greek word *exagoridzo*, which is a compound of the Greek words *ex* and *agoradzo*. The word *ex* means *out*; the word *agoradzo* means *"I buy."* When these words come together to form the word *exagoridzo*, it means *to buy back, to redeem, or to make the most of.* By using this word, Paul was telling the Ephesian believers, "Even though you've lost time because of your ungodly behavior, God is giving you the opportunity to buy back the time you've wasted."

Putting the meanings of all these words together, here is the *Renner Interpretive Version (RIV)* of Ephesians 5:16:

> **Buy back the time you've lost and make the most of each opportunity you still have.**

When we come to verse 17, Paul began his instructions on how to buy back the time. He said, "Wherefore be ye not unwise, but understanding what the will of the Lord is" (Ephesians 5:17). The word "unwise" is the Greek word *aphron*, which means *unintelligent* or *brainless*. And the word "understanding" in Greek is *suniemi*, and it describes *a coming together* and carries the idea of *putting all the pieces together, like putting together the many pieces of a jigsaw puzzle to reveal the big picture.*

Putting the meanings of all these words together, here is the *Renner Interpretive Version (RIV)* of Ephesians 5:17:

Don't be brainless; bring all the pieces together to see and understand the big picture of what God wants to do in life.

What is the "will of the Lord" Paul wanted them to understand? We find the answer in Ephesians 5:18: "And be not drunk with wine, wherein is excess; but be filled with the Spirit." Notice the word "drunk." It is the Greek word *methusko*, which means *to excessively drink alcohol or to be intoxicated*; it describes *a drunkard*. Apparently, the people in the church of Ephesus were drinking to the point of getting drunk. When Paul said, "And be not drunk with wine," it is a very strong prohibition in the Greek, which literally means, "Stop it! Stop it now! Put an end to this drunkenness. Your drinking is excessive."

Instead of being drunk with wine, Paul commanded them — *and us* — to "...be filled with the Spirit" (Ephesians 5:18). The word "filled" here is the Greek word *pleroo*, and it means *to fill to capacity; to fill to the full*. The tense here indicates *perpetual activity — be BEING filled*. Hence, we are to be continually filled with the Holy Spirit. It is an empowerment you are meant to experience every day.

What It Means To Receive a Fresh 'Supply' of the Spirit

Paul had personally experienced the empowering presence of the Holy Spirit on many occasions. On one of those occasions, he was confined to a dark, dank prison cell in the city of Rome. From there he wrote to the Philippian believers and said, "For I know that this shall turn to my salvation through your prayer, and the supply of the Spirit of Jesus Christ" (Philippians 1:19).

The word "supply" here is the Greek word *epichorégia*, and it describes *a lavish provision; an outrageously large contribution; a massive contribution*. This word was only used one other time in history. Paul knew about its original use and meaning and chose it for that reason. *Epichorégia* is a compound of two Greek words: the word *epi*, which means *on behalf of*, and the word *chorégia*, which is the word for *a choir, a chorus,* or *a chorography*. In the ancient world there was a huge choral group that had been preparing and training diligently to take their show on the road. And just when it was time for them to begin performing, the director of the group came and informed everyone that they were out of money. "You can pack your bags and go home," he said. "The show is over." This was a very dark moment for all of them.

A very wealthy man heard about their situation and how discouraged and defeated the choral members were. Moved with compassion, he came forward and made *a huge contribution on behalf of the choir* — which in Greek is the word *epichorégia*. He gave so much money to the group that when they received his contribution, it re-energized and empowered them to take their show back on the road and perform. This is the same word Paul used in Philippians 1:19, which is translated as "supply."

Paul was telling us that when we're in a dark, discouraging moment and it seems as though we're totally depleted of strength and resources to go on, it is the perfect moment to be refilled with the Holy Spirit! Jesus was Paul's wealthy benefactor and He is our wealthy benefactor too! He stands ready, willing, and able to refill you with the fullness of His Spirit. That's what you need, and it is yours for the asking!

In Philippians 1:20, Paul went on to say, "According to my earnest expectation and my hope, that in nothing I shall be ashamed, but that with all boldness, as always, so now also Christ shall be magnified in my body, whether it be by life, or by death." The word "magnified" here is the Greek word *megaluno*, which means *to amplify; boost; enlarge; expand; increase;* or *make great*. Paul received a fresh infilling of the Holy Spirit and believed he was amplified and boosted in his body with an exceeding supply of power and that he would make it out of the prison he was in.

Friend, to stay strong spiritually every day, *pray to be refilled with the Holy Spirit*. Whatever dark, difficult place you're in, it's no match for the power of Jesus! It's time for you to say, "Lord Jesus, I need a new infilling of the Holy Spirit. I welcome You to be my wealthy benefactor who steps forward in this moment and provides me with an enormous spiritual contribution that picks me up and puts me back on the road to my destiny in You. I ask this in Your Name Jesus, Amen!"

STUDY QUESTIONS

Study to shew thyself approved unto God, a workman that needeth
not to be ashamed, rightly dividing the word of truth.
— 2 Timothy 2:15

1. Carefully read Paul's warnings to the Ephesian believers — *and us* — in Ephesians 4:25-32 and identify the "foolish, brainless" behaviors they were exhibiting that he told them to stop. Are you struggling with any of these same attitudes or actions? If so, which ones? How does Paul urge us to act in instead?

2. In John 14:26 and 16:12-15, Jesus talked about the Person of the Holy Spirit just before going to the Cross. In what specific ways did He say you can expect the Spirit to help you every day? When you're overwhelmed and don't know what to pray, how does the Spirit step in and assist you? (*See* Romans 8:26,27.)

3. Throughout the book of Acts, when people received the baptism of the Holy Spirit, they began to speak in other tongues. Have you received this special prayer language from God? If so, are you using it daily? According to First Corinthians 14:4 and Jude 1:20, what can you expect to happen when you pray in tongues?

PRACTICAL APPLICATION

But be ye doers of the word, and not hearers only,
deceiving your own selves.
—James 1:22

1. As you come to the end of this study on the *Seven Things To Do Every Day To Stay Spiritually Strong*, what is one of your greatest takeaways? Of the seven things, which ones are already parts of your daily life? Which one(s) do you need to begin incorporating immediately?

2. As a believer, the Holy Spirit is living inside of you. He came and took up residence the moment you repented of sin and made Jesus the Lord of your life (*see* Galatians 4:6; John 14:23; 1 John 3:24). The *baptism in the Holy Spirit* is a separate experience that empowers you for God's service. Have you been baptized in the Spirit? If so, take a few moments to describe your experience.

3. If you have not received the baptism in the Holy Spirit — or would like to have a fresh infilling — take time now to pray and ask Jesus to baptize you with His Holy Spirit (*see* Jesus' words in Luke 11:9-13).

Notes

Notes

Notes

.

www.ingramcontent.com/pod-product-compliance
Lightning Source LLC
Chambersburg PA
CBHW071759020426
42331CB00008B/2318